THE WISDOM

of the

SUFI SAGES

TIMOTHY FREKE

ℑE

First published in 1998 by Journey Editions, an imprint of
Periplus Editions (HK) Ltd., with editorial offices at
153 Milk Street, Boston, Massachusetts 02109.

Distributed by:
USA
Charles E. Tuttle Co., Inc. RR 1 Box 231-5
North Clarendon, VT 05759
Tel.: (802) 773-8930 Fax.: (802) 773-6993

Japan
Tuttle Shokai Ltd. 1-21-13, Seki
Tama-ku, Kawasaki-shi
Kanagawa-ken 214
Japan
Tel.: (044) 833-0225 Fax.: (044) 822-0413

Southeast Asia
Berkeley Books Pte. Ltd. 5 Little Road #08-01
Singapore 536983
Tel.: (65) 280-3320 Fax.: (65) 280-6290

ISBN 1-885203-57-8
The Catalog Card Number is on file with
the Library of Congress

Printed in Hong Kong

CONTENTS

INTRODUCTION

"As-salaamu alaikum"

*"Peace to you,
from my heart
to your heart"*

Sufis are Muslim mystics who trace their spiritual lineage to the great prophet Muhammad, the founder of Islam. Like all mystics, Sufis are not concerned with secondhand knowledge about God, but with a personal experience of God. For Sufis, the outer forms of religion are merely vehicles for the spiritual content that lies beyond all rites and creeds. The

Sufi sage Shibli is said to have run through the streets carrying flaming coals announcing he was going to set fire to the Ka'aba, the most sacred place in Islam, so that Muslims would concern themselves less with a place and more with the Lord of the Ka'aba. Such enthusiasm for Truth has often caused Sufis to be branded as heretics, and horribly persecuted by orthodox Islamic authorities. Yet their wisdom has survived to inspire generations of spiritual seekers.

Sufism is a voyage of discovery into ourselves and beyond ourselves: a pilgrimage to become the perfect servants of Allah: a love affair with the Divine Beloved in which the lovers merge in mystical union. The Sufis may seem esoteric and mystifying, but actually they are trying to point us to something so obvious that we miss it. God is everywhere and everything. We are God. There is nothing but the Oneness of God. It is only our own sense of being a separate ego that obscures the omnipresent Truth. Sufism is simply about seeing things as they truly are – a mystical realization that is available to all. When the Sufi saint Rabi'a heard Salih of Qazwin teaching "Knock and the Door will open for you" she admonished him, "What are you talking about Salih, the Door has never been shut." The great mystic poet Jalaluddin Rumi wrote, "I knocked and the door opened, but I found I'd been knocking from the inside."

ı Allah

The Sufis approach God through many divine Names that express his various attributes, but the Name "Allah" combines and transcends all these attributes. Allah is the Supreme Reality. The word "Allah" combines the roots "al" and "la" to express "The Oneness of Being and Nothingness." God embraces all opposites. As it says in the Holy Qur'an "He is the first and the last, the apparent and the hidden." He is the "Soul of all souls" as Rumi puts it. He is not confined by any one creed but is the one God who speaks through all genuine religion, manifesting Himself in different ways appropriate to the individual seeker.

> *I have never known Allah, may He be exalted, except through the coincidence in Him of all opposites.*
>
> ABU SA'ID AL-KHARRAZ

66 Allah is non-being and being, existence and
non-existence. He is the relative and the Absolute.
All these concepts return to Allah, for there is
nothing we can comprehend or write or speak
about that is not Allah 99

ABD AL-KADER

11

Whatever you think concerning Allah –
know that he is different from that!

ABD AL-KADER

*Everything is a signpost
to the Oneness of Allah.*

AHMAD LBN ATA'ALLAH

*Saying "Allah Akbar" – "God is Most
Great" – doesn't mean he is greater
than something else, because there is
nothing else for Him to be greater than.
It means that he is too great to be
perceived by the senses and too deep to
be understood by the intellect. Too
great, indeed, to be known by anything
other than Him. Only God knows God.*

AHMAD LBN ATA'ALLAH

*God is nearer to man
than the jugular vein.*

QUR'AN 50.16

13

" God is your mirror in which you contemplate yourself and you are His mirror in which He contemplates his divine attributes. "

LBN ARABI

" God said, "To reveal the secrets of my abundant love, I created a mirror whose face is consciousness and whose back is the world." "

JALALUDDIN RUMI

❝ You've no idea
how hard I've looked for a gift to bring You.
Nothing seemed right.
What's the point of bringing gold to a gold mine,
or water to the ocean.
Everything I came up with
was like taking spices to the Orient.
It's no good giving my heart and soul,
because You already have these.
So – I've brought you a mirror.
Look at Yourself and remember me. ❞

JALALUDDIN RUMI

15

66 God is not limited to the way he appears to you by making Himself appropriate to your ability to receive Him. Therefore, no other creatures are obliged to obey the God you worship, for He appears to them in other forms. 99

IBN ARABI

66 Don't hang on exclusively to any particular creed so that you disbelieve the rest, or you will disregard much that is good and miss the real Truth. Allah is omnipotent and omnipresent and is not contained by any one religion, for he says in the Qur'an "Wherever you turn, there is the face of Allah." 99

IBN ARABI

66 The mystics speak in a hundred different ways, but if God is one and the Way is one, how could their meaning be other than one? What appears in different disguises is one essence. A variety of forms, but a unity of substance. 99

JALALUDDIN RUMI

How wonderful! A garden in the fire.
My heart transmutes itself to all forms;
a meadow for wild gazelles,
a monastery for Christian monks,
a temple for Pagan idols,
the Ka'aba for Muslim pilgrims,
tablets for the Jewish Law,
and pages for the Qur'an.
I proclaim the religion of Love,
and wherever it carries me,
this is my creed and my faith.

IBN ARABI

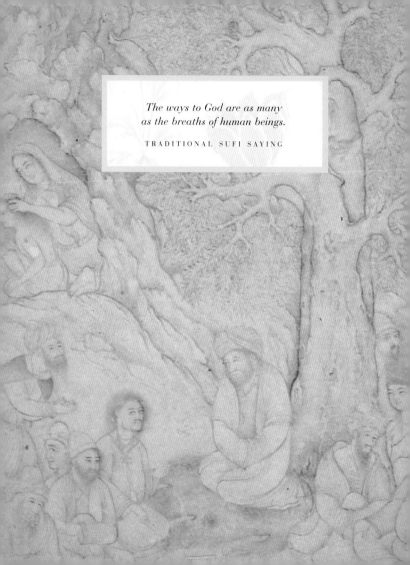

*The ways to God are as many
as the breaths of human beings.*

TRADITIONAL SUFI SAYING

ff A madman passed as a muezzin was giving the call
to prayer. The madman said, "That man up there is shaking
an empty nutshell." This is what you are doing when you
talk of the ninety-nine Names of Allah. How can God be
understood through names? You cannot use words to
describe the essence of God, so best to say nothing at all. ™™

KITAB-ILAHI

ff When "I" and "You" are absent,
I've no idea if this is a mosque,
synagogue, church, or temple. ™™

MAHMUD SHABISTARI

II The Sufi Path

The name "Sufi" is said to derive from the word for "wool," a reference to the coarse clothes worn by Muhammad and his early followers. It symbolizes humility, simplicity, and purity, that are important virtues on the Sufi path to God. Others say the name "Sufi" derives from the Greek word for wisdom. Although many great Sufis have been influential intellectuals, Sufi wisdom reaches beyond the mind to an intuitive apprehension of the Truth. As a traditional saying puts it, "The Sufis understand with the heart what the most learned scholars cannot understand with the head."

Sleep with the remembrance of death
and rise with the awareness
that you will not live long.

UWAIS EL-QARNI

❝ One thing must not be forgotten. Forget all else,
but remember this, and you'll have no regrets. Remember
and be concerned with everything else, but ignore this one
thing, and you'll have done nothing. It is as if a king has
sent you on a mission to a foreign land to perform one
specific task for him. If you do a hundred things, but not
this appointed task, what have you accomplished? Human
beings come into this world for a particular purpose, and if
they forget it they will have done nothing at all. ❞

JALALUDDIN RUMI

      A miser who had accumulated great riches decided he would take a year off to enjoy himself, when suddenly the Angel of Death appeared before him. The miser argued vehemently that he should be allowed to live, but the Angel began pulling him away. The miser then said, "Give me just a few more years and I will give you a third of all I possess," but the Angel refused. The miser said, "Give me just a few more days and I will give you half my wealth," but the Angel refused. The miser begged, "Give me a single day and I will give you all I own," but the Angel refused. Finally the miser sobbed. "Give me just long enough to write one thing down." The Angel agreed to this request and the miser wrote in his own blood, "Dear friends, value your lifetime. I could not buy a single moment more with all the money in my possession."

ATTAR

Do you want to be a pilgrim
on the path of Love?
The first step is making yourself
humble as ashes.

ANSARI OF HERAT

> *There is nothing better than to be without everything – no theories or practices. When you are without all, you will be with all.*
>
> BAYAZID AL-BISTAMI

Here's a tale: A soul was questioned by
God at the gates of Heaven,
"You are the same as when you left! You
were blessed by a life full
of opportunity – so where are
the bruises and scars left by
your journey?"

JALALUDDIN RUMI

Allah has a garden in this world.
Those who enter do not yearn
for the garden of the world to come.

AHMAD IBN ATA'ALLAH

OK – so I left the mosque and
went to the alehouse!
The sermon was interminably long,
and valuable time was wasting away.

HAFIZ

66 Embrace all creatures with love.
Don't say, "This inanimate thing has no awareness."
It does – it is you who have no awareness!
Let all things be as they are, and be kind to them
with the love of the Creator
in the midst of His creation. **99**

AHMAD LBN ATA'ALLAH

66 If you are more pleased when someone says
what a good person you are than when they say
what a bad person you are, then you are still
a bad person. **99**

SUFYAN ATH-THAWRI

> *Sufism is Truth without form.*
>
> LBN JALALI

❝ People who think anyone is lower than
themselves still have pride. **❞**

BAYAZID AL-BISTAMI

❝ Beware of the dangers of fame.
Live among ordinary folk
and don't seek to be a somebody. **❞**

BAYAZID AL-BISTAMI

> *The truly sincere act is one that*
> *is unknown to any recording angel,*
> *has no demon to oppose it,*
> *and no self to take pride in it.*
>
> ABU-YAQUB AL-SUSI

When Loqman was asked from whom he learnt
goodness, he replied, "From those without
goodness, because what seemed unbecoming in
them I avoid doing myself."

SA'DI

66 God said, "I appear uniquely to each of my servants. What each one imagines me to be, I become. Listen my servants, I am enclosed within these images. Purify your thoughts, for these are my home. Then see for yourself what is best for you – crying, laughing, fasting, or praying – and do whatever will best lead you onward." 99

JALALUDDIN RUMI

Children on the path drink the milk of the Qur'an and understand only its literal sense. The mature have their own understanding of its inner significance.

JALALUDDIN RUMI

66 A King was frightened to learn from his studies of astrology that a great calamity would soon befall him, so he built a room of solid rock to hide within and surrounded it by guards. When he was in it, he noticed a little chink of light that he filled in to prevent any harm reaching him. Thus he became a prisoner and died in that room. 99

ATTAR

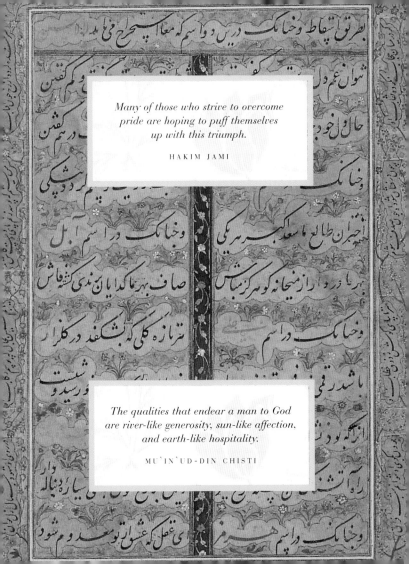

Many of those who strive to overcome
pride are hoping to puff themselves
up with this triumph.

HAKIM JAMI

The qualities that endear a man to God
are river-like generosity, sun-like affection,
and earth-like hospitality.

MU'IN'UD-DIN CHISTI

" A man stole some fruit from a tree. The owner reprimanded him, "That is unlawful, do you not fear God?" The man replied, "Why should I? The tree belongs to God and I am God's servant eating fruit from His tree." The owner picked up a stick and started beating him. The man yelled, "How can you treat me like this? Do you not fear God?" The owner replied, "Why should I? You are a servant of God and this stick that belongs to God is being used to strike God's servant." "

SUFI TEACHING STORY

Sell your cleverness and buy bewilderment.
Cleverness is mere opinion.
Bewilderment brings intuitive knowledge.

JALALUDDIN RUMI

" Perplexity increases as the descent of the divine increases, but this is the source of spiritual knowledge. This is why the Prophet, on Him be grace and peace, said, "Allah, swell my perplexity in relationship to You!" "

ABD AL-KADER

The path is the service of others,
not prayer beads and dervish robes.

SA'DI

Self-justification is worse
than the original offence.

ZIAUDIN

A saint who thinks he is a saint
is no longer a saint.

TRADITIONAL SAYING

When does a man become a man?
When he knows his own mistakes
and hurries to correct them.

BAYAZID AL-BISTAMI

Someone who seeks God through
logical proof is like someone
who looks for the sun with a lamp

TRADITIONAL SUFI SAYING

The search has no final finding,
Knowledge of God is without end.

ABD AL-KADER

A path has no value
when you've arrived.

HUJWIRI

The world exists only as an appearance;
from beginning to end
it is a playful game.

SHABISTARI

“ A greedy Caliph was very attached to his wealth,
so the Sufi sage Shaqiq asked him, "Would you give one
half of your kingdom to someone who could provide you
with a drink of water if you were in the desert dying of
thirst?" The Caliph said he would. Shaqiq then asked,
"Would you give the other half of your kingdom to
someone able to help you pass that water if you had
become unable to do so?" The Caliph agreed he would.
"Why then do you value your kingdom so highly,"
asked Shaqiq, "when you would give it away in return
for a drink of water which would itself not even
stay with you?" ”

SUFI TEACHING STORY

III Remembrance
and Surrender

The word "Islam" means "surrender." At the heart of Sufism is complete submission of the personal will to the will of God. This can be accomplished through "Zikr" or "remembering God," for as Allah says in the *Holy Qur'an*, "Remember Me and I will remember you." By being aware of God everywhere and at all times, Sufis dissolve their personal identities into the Divine. They then experience that there is and only ever has been the Oneness of Allah. Allah is the consciousness that sees, acts, and lives through all beings. Everything that happens is actually an expression of the will of Allah, who is all and does all.

> ❝ Hearts find peace
> In the remembrance of God ❞
>
> QUR'AN 13.28

*The hearts of those at the end of the
path are occupied continually with
the remembrance of God.*

AHMAD LBN ATA'ALLAH

*The Sufi is pleased with everything
that God does, so that God will be
pleased with all that he does.*

ABU SA'ID LBN ABI-L-KHAYR

*I won't serve God like
a laborer expecting wages.*

RABI'A

*All your suffering comes from desiring
things that cannot be had. Stop desiring
and you won't suffer.*

JALALUDDIN RUMI

The true mystic is not a devotee lost
in ecstatic communion with the One,
or a reclusive saint who avoids others. The true mystic
lives alongside other people – coming and going, eating
and sleeping, buying and selling, marrying and chatting
– but not for a moment does he forget God.

ABU SA'ID IBN ABI-L-KHAYR

Wherever you find yourself, whether in worship or in
ordinary life, contemplate God – in what you eat,
what you drink, whom you marry, always aware that
he is both the Contemplated and the Contemplator.

ABD AL-KADER

Invoke the all-embracing Name that is Allah,
Allah, Allah. But don't violate this remembrance
by letting your tongue pronounce His Name while
something else is in your heart. Let your heart speak
and your ear witness, until the speaker becomes
your true Self.

AHMAD IBN ATA'ALLAH

" A tablet has to be wiped clean before it can be written on again. One heart cannot contain two things. If it is filled with the appearances of the senses, it is rare that it will know the meaning of Allah, even if it repeated "Allah" a thousand times. But say "Allah" once with the heart empty of everything that is not God, and you will find a bliss beyond the tongue to tell. "

AHMAD LBN ATA'ALLAH

Praying sincerely is a high risk venture.
You must wager your self and hope to lose.

When you strip off your self-image,
there is no devotion or devotee.

Lover and Beloved are united,
in the light of your eyes.

MAHMUD SHABISTARI

" When you realise the mystery of Oneness with
the Divine, you will know that you are no other
than God, and that you have always been and
will always be beyond every time and place.
Then you will understand that all your actions
are His actions, and your essence is His essence,
and all your attributes belong to Him.

The soul then understands that it does not see
God through itself but through God, so that it is
not the soul which loves God but God who loves
Himself. The soul sees God in all beings,
but only because it is God who is looking.
He is lover and beloved, seeker and sought. "

IBN ARABI

*The one that brought me here,
will have to take me home.*

JALALUDDIN RUMI

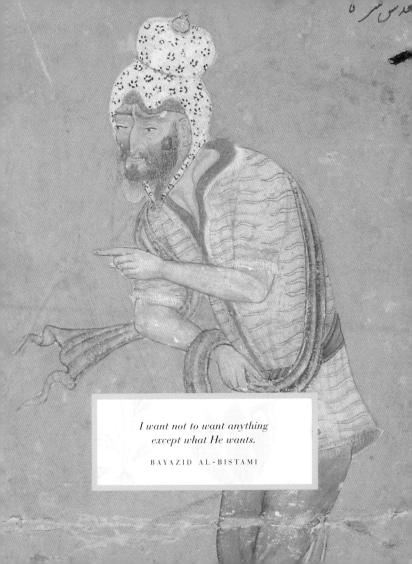

I want not to want anything
except what He wants.

BAYAZID AL-BISTAMI

> There are three signs of a sound love of the Lord:
> lack of self will, pleasure in every event that happens by
> divine decree, and, by seeing the perfection of the Beloved
> in all things, resting content through surrender to Him.

AHMAD LBN ATA'ALLAH

> The mystic is the knower without knowledge.
> The mystics are not themselves, but exist in God.
> Their actions are God's actions. Their words are
> God's words uttered by their tongues. Their sight is
> God seeing through their eyes.

DHU'L-NUN

66 God brought me into his Presence and asked, "Bayazid,
how did you come to Me?" I replied, "By renouncing the
world." He said, "The world is worth a mosquito's wing,
how did renouncing this bring you here?" I said, "Forgive
me, I came to You through dependence on You." God said,
"Did I ever betray that trust which I assured you of?"
I said, "Forgive me, I came to You through You."
Then God said, "Now we embrace." 99

BAYAZID AL-BISTAMI

IV · The Lovers

······ ✳ ······

Before the time of Muhammad, the Arabs used the term "shair," which means "knower," to refer to people with profound spiritual knowledge. Such people were often believed to be possessed by spirits. Later "shair" came to mean "poet." Many of the great Sufis have been poets whose verses overflow with divine inspiration. To express the intensity of their longing for God and the ecstasy of their communion with God they turn to metaphors of intoxication and romantic love. For such Sufis God is not a distant Lord of the Universe; he is an intimate Friend. He is their Beloved with whom they share a passionate, sacred love affair.

> *Love calls – everywhere and always.*
> *We're sky bound. Are you coming?*
>
> JALALUDDIN RUMI

The Lovers are a sect distinct
from all others;
with a faith and creed all of their own.

JALALUDDIN RUMI

If you are for real,
risk everything for love.
If not – get out of here!
Half a heart isn't enough.
You keep setting out to find God,
but end up spending more time
in run down wayside taverns.

JALALUDDIN RUMI

I'm drunk with Love.
Neither now-here nor nowhere.
I'm incapable of anything
but celebration.

JALALUDDIN RUMI

> I drank it down in one
> and collapsed intoxicated by purity.
> Ever since, I can't tell if I exist or not.
> Sometimes I know the bliss
> of the "I" that looks through my eyes.
> Other times my habits dump me back in the shit.
> But then there it is – that aroma once again.
> I'm returned to the Rose Garden.

JALALUDDIN RUMI

> My heart brimming with Your hope is the rarest of riches.
> My tongue tasting Your Name is the sweetest of flavors.
> Moments passed with you transcends time.
> I am a lonesome stranger in Your world.
> This is why I am complaining.

RABI`A

Ah, my Beloved, fill the cup that clears
Today of past regret and future fears –
Tomorrow? – Why tomorrow I may be
Myself with yesterdays sev'n thousand years.

OMAR KHAYYAM

She embraced me in the night.
My idol entwined me in Her arms.
She captured me and pierced me
with a ring that showed I was her slave.
I exclaimed, "For this loving I'll cry, I'll rage, I'll frenzy..."
but she closed my mouth with Her sweet lips.

HAMADANI

Dreaming – I am with Her,
lips locked to lips,
body bound to body.

I sigh, "Let now be always,"
but when I wake again
I am outside knocking on Her door.

HAMADANI

Chained by love.
Captured again.
Struggle is futile.
Escape is impossible.

Love is a sea
with unseen shores –
with no shores at all.
The wary don't dive in.
To swim in love
is to drink poison
and find it sweet.

I struggled like a wild mare
drawing the noose tighter.

RABI'A

v Fana and Ittihad

······· ✤ ·······

This ego-self is only a mask obscuring our true divine identity. The goal of Sufism is "fana fi Allah," extinction of the separate self in the Oneness of Allah. This voluntary death is no loss, however, because this self is only an illusion. Allah is the only Reality. When the Sufi abandons his illusionary self he enters a blissful state of "ittihad" or mystical union, in which he is one with God. Ibn Arabi teaches that God created human beings so that through them He could come to know Himself. When the Sufi sage attains "ittihad," God recognizes Himself.

> *The true lover finds the light only if*
> *he is his own fuel and, like a candle,*
> *consumes himself.*
>
> ATTAR

The Moon was asked. "What is your greatest wish?"
It answered. "That the sun should remain always
obscured by clouds. or disappear altogether."

SUFI TEACHING STORY

*You yourself are your own obstacle
– rise above yourself.*

HAFIZ

66 There are two types of death. One which is inevitable
and common to all, and one which is voluntary and
experienced by the few. It is the second death which the
Messenger of Allah prescribed saying, "Die before you die."
Those who die this voluntary death are resurrected. All the
business of their lives return to the Oneness of God. They
see God through God. As the Prophet said, on Him be grace
and peace, "You will not see your Lord until you are dead."
This is because it is through this death and resurrection that
everything becomes nothing and only One thing exists – One
Reality. For initiates, whatever will befall a believer after
physical death is prefigured in this life. This return of the
many forms of things to Allah and the end of their
becoming, is only a change in perception not in the Reality.
For someone who dies and attains resurrection, the many
are One through an essential Unity, and the One is many
through His many aspects and their relationships. 99

ABD AL-KADER

*You are a droplet of water
from an infinite ocean.*

HAJI BAHAUDIN

“ I didn't take a single footstep toward God
by being with the pious, or the warriors in the cause,
or those who pray excessively. So I asked, "God,
how can I reach You?" God said, "Leave your self
behind and come." ”

BAYAZID AL-BISTAMI

“ A man knocked on a door. "Who is there?" asked God.
"Me," replied the man. "Go away then," said God.
The man left and wandered in the arid desert until he
realized his error and returned to the door.
He knocked again. "Who's there?" asked God.
"You," answered the man. "Then come in,"
replied God. "There's no room here for two." ”

SUFI TEACHING STORY

Love is to stand before your Beloved,
striped naked of all attributes,
so that His qualities become your
qualities.

AL-HALLAJ

Don't think you are veiled from Allah
by something that is not Allah.
There is nothing besides Allah.
You are veiled form Him by the
illusion that there is something
other than Allah.

AHMAD IBN ATA'ALLAH

Someone called out, "I'm looking for
Bayazid," Bayazid replied, "I have also
been searching for 'Bayazid' for thirty
years, and still have not found him."

SUFI TEACHING STORY

66 The Sufi saint al-Hallaj was crucified for daring to proclaim "I am God." One of the orthodox who participated in his murder later had a dream in which he saw the great saint being ceremoniously welcomed into Heaven. Confused by this, he asked God, "Oh Lord! Why was pharaoh condemned to the flames for proclaiming 'I am God' and al-Hallaj is ushered into Heaven for speaking the same words?" A divine voice answered, "When pharaoh spoke these words he thought only of himself and had forgotten Me. But when al-Hallaj spoke these same words he had forgotten himself and thought only of Me. Therefore 'I am God' in pharaoh's mouth was a curse to him, but in al-Hallaj's mouth this 'I am God' was due to my grace." 99

SUFI TEACHING STORY

God has stolen my false "I" and brought
me close to the true "I." All colors have
returned to pure white. The journey is over
and nothing but God exists. All attributes
and relationships have been erased.
The primal state has been reestablished.

ABD AL-KADER

One second I was trapped in dark narrow fear.
Suddenly I am no longer confined by the universe.
Even if every hair could say "thank you,"
I would be unable to express my gratitude.
I say it over and over again – I say nothing else –
"If only everyone could know what I know."

JALALUDDIN RUMI

There is only One Light,
and "you" and "me"
are holes in the lamp shade.

MAHMUD SHABISTARI

You search for the one who is with you.
You look for the looker –
closer to you than you.
Don't rush outside.
Thaw like melting ice,
and wash your self away.

JALALUDDIN RUMI

When you lose yourself,
you find the Beloved.
There is no other secret.
I don't know any more than this.

ANSARI OF HERAT

" In the state of fana. which is also called ittihad.
Lord and worshiper. lover and Beloved. both disappear.
If there is no lover there is no Beloved. If there is no devotee
there is no Lord. The two are an inseparable polarity, so the
disappearance of one is the disappearance of the other. "

ABD AL-KADER

Don't say, "I am nothing,"
but don't say, "I am something."
Don't say, "Nothing concerns me,"
but don't say, "Something concerns me."
Just say, "Allah" –
and you will witness wonders.

SIDI ALI AL-JAMAL

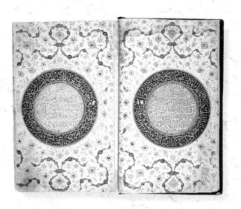

66 Don't think that saying "I am God" is proclaiming one's greatness. It is actually total humility. Some one who says, "I am the servant of God" infers two – God and himself – whereas someone who says, "I am God" negates himself. He relinquishes his own existence. "I am God" means "I don't exist. Everything is God. Only God exists. I am nothing. I am utter emptiness." This is complete humility not arrogance, but people often misunderstand. When someone says he is God's servant, he still sees himself as a doer, albeit in God's service. He is not yet drowned in the ocean of God. When he is, there will be no such thing as "his actions," only movements of the water. 99

JALALUDDIN RUMI

The publishers would like to thank the following for the use of pictures:

Bridgeman Art Library: pp. 27, 38, 52, 57
e.t. archive: pp. 8, 12, 17, 18, 19, 21, 23, 25, 29, 37, 41, 42, 51, 54, 59, 60
Vanessa Fletcher: pp. 11, 14, 15, 33, 44, 45, 49